IMPROVE YOUR TENNIS IN 4 WEEKS

Tennis for Mind & Body

Bob Seshadri

ISBN-13: 9798461198770
ISBN-10: 1477123456

Cover design by: Art Painter
Library of Congress Control Number: 2018675309
Printed in the United States of America

This book is dedicated to my mother. She made sure I continued to play tennis and complete my education after the demise of my father. This book is also dedicated to the light of my life and my biggest fan, my daughter Krithika, to Alex my son in law, a constant motivator by my side and my loving tolerant wife Prema.

"Always believe in yourself and never give up, because you don't know what success could be right around the corner."

JAMIE HAMPTON

CONTENTS

INTRODUCTION
Improve your Tennis in 4 Weeks

Yes, I mean it. You will improve your game in 4 weeks flat. All you need to do is follow the instructions and practice daily.

I wrote this book to help amateurs, and recreational self-taught aspirants, improve their skill set and enjoy the game. I would like them to be happy while they play and leave the court pleasantly exhausted and relaxed after a decent game. I have addressed almost all challenges faced by a recreational player as detailed in the next chapter.

In this book the reader will be taken through every aspect of the game starting from the selection process of a tennis racket, through grips for different strokes, the ideal practice drills and last but not least, on and off-court Tennis Ettiquates. Watching players struggling with their strokes, trying to emulate pros on the tennis circuit triggered off my desire to write this book. The observations included amateurs not being able to stroke the ball, cursing themselves, bashing the racket, and chucking the ball to the next court in frustration, begging the question, are they truly enjoying themselves?

The mental and emotional aspect of the game is a performance-determining factor in tennis, forming an integral part of the book. Four years back, at 65, playing tennis with my mates, I anticipated a drop shot coming to my backhand while I found myself on the far end of the forehand court. I started running towards the ball, I couldn't stop and went straight into the net, head over heels. The point I am making is while securing a point is part of the game at any age and level, we need to do that from a positive and sensible state of mind.

THE CHALLENGES
OF A RECREATIONAL
TENNIS PLAYER

The challenges are varied, depending on how the individual started playing the game, whether they were coached or self-taught. After interviewing several players, I arrived at the following list:

☺ Most players suffer from inconsistency in keeping the ball in play or getting their serve in at a decent speed.

☺ Despite all good intentions, the ball flies out of the court.

☺ The ball hits the bottom of the net.

☺ Some players are unable to reach the ball on time and end up reaching the ball too late.

☺ Some are unable to decide which grip suits them the best.

☺ Many forget to change their grip for different strokes.

☺ The majority choke up their second service during a game.

☺ Invariably most players cover their weak backhand.

☺ Most are reluctant to come up to the net.

☺ Many are not able to hit deep strokes.

☺ A background of wristy strokes inherited from other racket games ruin their tennis.

The reasons for all the above and more stem from a few areas.

Most recreational players start playing games much before they have learnt to stroke the ball correctly.

The objective in playing a game narrows down to hitting winners or use any method to secure the point.

You continue to hit a ball incorrectly in whichever way, the muscle memory will absorb and store those incorrect movements that you will find difficult to change.

Then some of us have learnt tennis on our own or by watching videos and may not have done so correctly. This too stops your natural style from developing. **The good news is you can learn tennis on your known and still play a decent game.**

When we imitate players we tend to use grips like they do and tend to injure ourselves. I have addressed all the challenges in this book for you to play the game without stressing or injuring yourself. The bottom line is quite simple. The more balls you hit during the practice sessions, the better you will get. So please pay attention to my chapter on practice.

The chapter on Practise sessions will make you fitter but do pay attention to your diet and practice physical fitness-oriented exercises that will strengthen your neck, wrist, arms, shoulders, chest, stomach, thigh, and calf muscles.

PROLOGUE

"THERE IS NO WAY AROUND HARD WORK, EMBRACE IT."- RALPH NADAL

MY JOURNEY WITH LAWN TENNIS

The year was 1960. I started playing tennis at eight. My parents were introduced to tennis when the Indian tennis legend Ramanathan Krishnan stayed with us in Calcutta escorted by Dr Rajan from Madras, India. Having played on clay courts all his life the first exposure to the lawns of Calcutta South Club was a new experience, as I heard from my late mother. Lawn courts are much faster than clay, and it takes a while to get used to both surfaces.

My introduction to lawn courts happened at a Tennis Club close to home. I was escorted to the club by my mother. I started playing with a Dunlop Max-Ply wooden racket, that I would dutifully place back into the wooden frame, to protect the wood from warping. My father, a Provincial Controller with Bata Shoe Company, passed on by the time I was 10, and my mom saw me through tennis and education.

I grew up watching players like Roy Emerson, Rod Laver, Bob Hewitt, Fred Stole, John Newcombe, Barry Mackay with the big serve, Ismeil El Shafei with the double-handed backhand. I have played with Ion Tiriac, Alex Metraveli, Ille Nastase, Billy Knight and a few others whose names I have forgotten. Today's tennis is different to touch play. We see excellent players with admirable body and mind fitness, power rallying on both clay and lawn courts combined with intelligent strategizing.

I picked up the game faster than expected and soon had joined the Bengal lawn Tennis Association (BLTA). There were three or four grades, Grade A, being the group for the best players. I joined Group B and moved up to A within a few months. BLTA used Calcutta South Club and Saturday Club Courts to train the young aspirants. The late Stanley Edwards was our coach, later replaced by Akhtar Ali. While Calcutta South Club had both lawns and Hard Courts, Saturday Club had the reddish hard courts. These courts had red soil whereas the clay courts in Southern India had brown clay courts that were even slower than the red courts of Calcutta. I soon got used to both surfaces and adapted my style of playing.

Calcutta was known for its tennis fan following. There were several ranking tournaments, starting from Calcutta Hard Court played at The South Club, the floodlit tournaments played at the Saturday Club, hard courts at the Ordnance Club, and Cossipore Club, and the lawns of Gymkhana Club. I started playing the tennis tournament circuits in India, experiencing the slow grey courts, in Madras, Hyderabad, and the lawns of Delhi, Allahabad, the hard courts of Bombay Gymkhana Club, Mussoorie, where my timing was shot to pieces due to the altitude and a few non recognized, non-ranking money-making tournaments at Vizag, Nellore and Anantapur in India. Unfortunately, I could never complete a full circuit as I had to come back home to attend school and university to complete my graduation as education in India is a priority to secure a decent job.

I went on to win the under 13 and 18 categories in West Bengal and played the inter-state tournaments. Then along with the lack of guidance came the distractions of teen age popularity, the tendency to give way to temptations, the need to work for a living, a bad motorcycle accident that left me with multiple fractures on my left leg heralding the end of competitive tennis for me.

MY CORPORATE JOURNEY

I have travelled extensively, coaching sales consultants in automotive dealerships, training Branch managers, visiting organizations in different parts of the world, observing their management structures, styles, negotiation methods, strategies, communication methodologies and particularly noticing their state of mind and attitudes towards work, recreational life and trying to draw out a work-life balance. Along with my tennis playing days with forays into golf, during the last decade, I unconsciously started drawing parallels between management strategies and the game.

◆ ◆ ◆

TENNIS FOR ALL

"WHEN YOU DO SOME-
THING BEST IN LIFE, YOU
DON'T WANT TO GIVE THAT
UP – AND FOR ME IT'S
TENNIS." —ROGER FEDERER

Tennis is also one of the games which take place in the mind. We play against our inner devils of nervousness, self-doubt, lack of concentration, and self-condemnation. During my daily 8-hour tennis routine, I used to wonder how there were times when I could do no wrong and days when everything went wrong. My coach Stanley Edwards spent a long time trying to get me out of a bad habit, of a looping forehand swing. Dear reader, be pleasantly warned, you will be going through this phase of unlearning and relearning process, and I request you to simply go through the motion.

A person with an attitude of 'I know it all' cannot learn anything. There is no life, no vitality in a person who is unwilling to learn or unlearn and start afresh. Open the windows of your mind and let the information flow in.

The common issues may include "I am aware of what to do but I just can't do what I should do! This is my horror story of golf! One tends to remember one part and forget the rest. Somedays they will all come together. The next day nothing will work. It is okay, let it be, do not stress. You are on the court to have a good time!

Do not let the instructions in this book send you into a tailspin. Read and absorb the knowledge and let your subconscious do the trick for you. The art of effortless concentration can not only deliver on the tennis court but in other spheres of your life.

So, what are you doing when you are correcting yourself by saying "bend your knees"? You have identified the error and are imprinting the thought in your head to help you not repeat the mistake. This will fructify if you do this without anger. Imagine the clearest possible picture of you hitting the ball with the right amount of bend in the knee and see the ball reach the desired space. When the mind is quiet and focused, things happen without effort.

I am sure you have experienced driving to work through heavy traffic with a million things playing out in your brain and realizing you are at your destination only when you switch off the ignition.

What happens to you when you recall the moment of your greatest achievement? How does that show up on your energy level? The same thing applies when you hit a good shot, reflect upon the winning stroke and prepare for the next. If you miss that shot, do not berate yourself but think about what you did incorrectly which sent the ball to the bottom of the net or outside the court.

Recall the times when you did not realize how you managed to reach the ball and hit an inconceivable shot. Something inside you will ignite and make you do things you thought you will never do.

Let me relate one of my experiences. It was an Inter-state tournament; my opponent had lobbed me deep to my forehand corner, I am a right-hander, I reached the ball and hit it back to my opponent's backhand (he was also a right-hander), he then placed a cross-court drop shot to my backhand close to the net and ran up. I got to the drop shot and placed a sharp backhand cross-court skimming the net. I came back to earth when I heard the applause from the crowd. I could not fathom how the whole thing happened, it just happened. I was in a different zone. Something inside you will ignite and make you do things that you thought you could never do. I had gone through the motions perfectly and thoughtlessly and was serving for the match.

What happens to us when a game has commenced? We start strategizing the game plan, judge our opponents, worrying whether we can afford to lose especially if you are ranked and the opponent is not, fearing the outcome of a loss, hoping for unforced errors from the opponent, trying too hard not to miss, regretting the last shot and choking.

Making room for imperfections in us is the first step. Outside the court making allowances for other's imperfections leads to compassion and empathy.

SELECTION OF RACKET

"I'LL LET THE RACKET DO THE TALKING"- JOHN MCENROE

Here is a quick tip for those who are going to venture out to secure a tennis racket for themselves.

Beginners can go with an "oversize" racket, it will help them to get that "sweet spot" and make contact with the ball consistently. The larger the racket head, the higher the power and lesser the control over the ball, and the inverse with smaller head size, you get better control but lesser power. Old-timers in tennis will appreciate when we moved from a wooden tennis racket to a graphite one we were hitting the ball all over the place as they generated more power. However, with a wider head, it is easier to get that sweet spot, the right place for the ball and racket to make contact.

Look at the grip size. It will be shown on the bottom of the grip. A smaller grip requires a tighter hold, you need to use more muscle power to prevent the grip from twisting. A grip that is too large prevents your wrist from snapping during a Serve. I prefer using a 4/5.8 as I have a large palm. The net is full of information. Even if you get a 4/3.8, you can add on a grip on your own, which will get you to a comfortable grip size. If you end up selecting too large a grip then that has to be shaved down, which is a more complicated task. Take your time about it, as even a small variation of a grip size can make a big difference to the way a racket performs. A smaller grip size gets you a higher spin.

Go for a weight that you are comfortable with, well balanced so that the racket head can be held up higher than your wrist without much effort. Those who want a better power on their Serve can go for a slightly top-heavy version. The downside is, if the racket head feels too heavy then you might end up dropping the racket head below the wrist which may lead to endless miseries.

Racket strings also play an important part. An open stringbed gives you more power and a denser stringbed gives you more control. I would recommend you go with a thought pattern of "control" over "power".

It is important to take time over the selection process. A racket is an extension of your arm on the tennis court. Don't rush.

STANCE

"REGARDLESS OF HOW YOU
FEEL INSIDE, ALWAYS TRY
TO LOOK LIKE A WINNER."

-ARTHUR ASHE

Stance

How do you wait for the ball? Most amateurs end up standing flat-footed with their feet firmly planted to the ground. What happens if you do that in your work front? You get inflexible, you cannot move fast enough if the situation demands it. You are waiting for disaster to reach you before you can react.

So, the idea is to be on your toes, shifting your weight from leg to leg, fully aware, focused, with your eye on the ball. The racket head is held at the neck with the non-playing arm, pointing straight ahead, above your wrist, and elbows out.

Your eyes must be on the ball from the time it leaves your opponent's racket through the time the ball meets your racket face and goes across the net to your opponent.

In the business world, market forces are constantly changing; you need to keep an eye on the market, your opponent and your product performance, all the time.

GRIPS

The shape of the racket handle is an octagon. Note the bevel on which the bottom knuckle of the index finger and the heel pad rest.

This is a much-discussed and controversial area. Most of you would have held the racket the way you feel most comfortable and started hitting the ball hoping it would cross the net. Once you get that right then it must have been the effort of not sending the ball hurtling out of the courts and get yelled at by your mates!

Here I will try to help with the grip you are already used to and leaving the change of grip as an option for you if you are seeking adventure and make life interesting!

The principal rule is to hold the racket firm and not hard.

Players may change their grip depending on the situation. When a player flattens their shot, they are moving their grip counterclockwise to achieve less topspin and more horizontal velocity.

If a player wants to hit a topspin lob, they move their grip clockwise. Racket head control, i.e., the grip, is one of the three basic variables of tennis, along with timing and balance. The newer grips seem to put unnatural stress on the arm.

Touch, placement, timing, and especially court anticipation are the reasons Federer is still beating most guys half his age!

Here are a few ways of holding the grip. A grip has an octagonal structure with eight bevels. The bevel areas are marked in the diagram for a better understanding of holding the grip.

CONTINENTAL GRIP – BEVELS 1 AND 2

Until the mid-1970s, most major tournaments in India and abroad were played on grass and the forehand grip of choice among the game's players. Although the popularity of this grip began to decline in the 1970s, players like John McEnroe, Martina Navratilova and Stefan Edberg continued to use the style.

When Rod Laver in the 1960s and '70s, was using the Continental grip it was ideal for grass courts. Points 1 & 2 should be within the cusp of your hand, with the thumb and the index finger giving the support to hold the racket firm. The grass produced low, skidding shots, and most players with wooden rackets those days, produced little spin. It was a flat stroked, serve and volley game.

Players would exchange minimum rallies which were largely knee-high shots and ran up to the net to avoid the unreliable grass bounces, and resort to angled or deep corner volleys to put away their opponents.

Only the slightest grip adjustments were required to hit any shot. Players who use the Continental grip included Margaret Court, John McEnroe, and Billy Jean King.

So, it is your choice if you want to use this grip for serves overheads, volleys and drop shots.

But as a continental forehand grip, it is no longer suited to today's high-speed, high-spin, high-bounce game. Today's market scenario demands, speed, marketing actions that are required in today's business environment and something that the competition will find difficult to match.

EASTERN GRIP
– BEVEL 3

 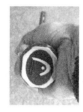

This is one of the most common grips that may help you to hit an effective flat forehand, and if you work on it you may end up hitting good top spins as well. On the way, you will probably end up hitting the ball to the bottom of the net due to your over-enthusiastic approach to spin the ball.

Imagine you are shaking hands with the racket. Look at the figure. Point #3 should be within the cusp of your hand, with the thumb and the index finger giving the support to hold the racket firm. You will end up with an eastern grip. Players who use the Eastern grip for their forehand include Chris Evert, Pete Sampras, Steffi Graf and Roger Federer.

Borg used an Eastern Grip and a tennis revolution started taking shape. He began imparting far more topspin on the ball than anyone else, hitting harder and harder shots that would dip down inside the opponent's baseline while his opponent waited for a deep shot.

The game moved back to the baseline as more power came into the game, fitness was of paramount importance and the message came through that a player could win by playing almost exclusively from the backcourt with hard and topspin shots.

Borg paired the Eastern grip with an upward, arcing swing path to create all that topspin.

While Pete Sampras used a perfect Eastern grip, Roger Federer's is a bit of a mix, as he shifts his grip further down to # 4 on the grip.

SEMI WESTERN GRIP – BEVEL 4

T he quest for more power and topspin led to the evolution of the tennis racket using fibreglass, larger racket head and string technology. Once you start hitting loopier, heavier topspin resulting in the ball bouncing up to the other guy's shoulder your opponent tends to do the same thing or lob the ball as we see in most senior club tennis.

For the Semi-Western grip, you need to move your hand another notch clockwise from the Eastern (or counterclockwise for left-handers). With this grip, you will be forced to move the hand and arm together to create the arc of the swing that creates tremendous topspin. This requires a lot of power and control. Many club players have tried it and end up in frustration or pain as it stresses out the arm and shoulders and the tendons. For today's shoulder-high bounces on artificial courts, the Semi-Western is well suited, allowing a player to more easily get the racket up and over the ball at contact to impart the spin. The contact point must always be in front of the players. Nadal, Serena Williams Novak Djokovic use this grip.

WESTERN GRIP – BEVEL 5

Khachanov, the 23-year-old Russian used his big serve and powerful Western-grip forehand to beat Djokovic in the 2018 Paris Masters.

Kyle Edmund and Jack Sock use the Western grip, placing their palm under the racket, Bevel #5, creating even greater topspin shots hit with immense power.

To increase your topspin and height of the bounce, this may be the ideal grip.

The downside is you will be constantly shifting grips for other strokes. However, this is the best grip for your backhand as you can topspin as well as slice and use it as a drop shot to the run-up to the net and be ready to volley if you wish to.

You can use any grip you want, that you are comfortable with. You will notice some of the game's best players have put their playing arm palm on one of the Bevels or a variation of two. Rafael Nadal, who plays left-handed, would be on Bevel 6 and very close to 5.

I believe pros that are teaching recreational/semi-competitive players to hit with topspin using a Western grip are doing many of them a disservice relegating them to a lifetime of inconsistency and injuries. This has given rise to the most miserable players on the courts are those that can't keep the ball in play and "beat themselves".

So the bottom line dear friends is that you can choose the grip that you are most comfortable with, and we will improve upon that.

A FOREHAND

"MY FAVOURITE SHOT IS ALWAYS GONNA BE THE FOREHAND. IT USED TO ALWAYS BE MY FAVOURITE SHOT WHEN I WAS YOUNG, SO ITS THE ONE I HAVE WON ALL THE POINTS WITH."- ROGER FEDERER

This is the first stroke that normally every person hits on the court. One cardinal rule is that the racket head must be higher than your wrist joint to provide you with leverage to control your stroke and return the ball.

The Grip for a Forehand Stroke

I recommend the Continental, or whatever grip you are comfortable with at the present moment and we will see how to get the best out of it. You have the option to hit flat, topspin or roll the ball, which is a combination of a flat stroke and a topspin.

The 'ready position' is the same for any stroke. It determines how the rest of the movements follow and finally the finish. Your eye is on the ball with your opponent. The ready position is standing on your toes shifting your weight between the two legs. So, the idea is to be on your toes, fully aware, focused, with your eye on the ball. The racket head is held at the neck with the non-playing arm, pointing straight ahead, above your wrist elbows out. It is the other way around if you are a left-hander. This is an important part as the non-stroking hand supports the racket weight, keeps the movement in the correct arc, and eases the tension on the playing hand.

The Torso Turn.

As soon as you see the ball leaving your opponent's racket, start turning your torso, hips, shoulder and arm to prepare for the backswing. Do not let your eye leave the ball.

I have always recommended the **classic** method of placing the left leg forward, (right-handers) pointing the left shoulder towards the ball and connecting with the ball with the racket head higher than the wrist swinging your shoulder, your hip and your body weight behind the ball for power. The non-playing hand moves across the body almost parallel to the baseline. This used to help me track the ball as well. In this method, you are using your body weight. You have better control over the ball in the classic stance.

However, you will see most major players these days using an **open stance** wherein you need to use more of your arm and shoulder power. The advantage of this stance is that you have the whole court in front of you to place the ball wherever you want.

When you rotate your body, you are automatically coiling the oblique muscles. While rotating your shoulder you are already moving your racket head to a ready position with your backswing to hit the ball. Getting ready early in this manner will stop you from waiting for the ball till the last second before beginning your backswing.

Stroking the ball.

Remember to keep your racket head higher than the wrist and then begin the downward swing uncoiling your torso, transferring your weight to the forward leg. It is ideal to have your knee almost in line with the ball, bending it to the height required. Many errors can be avoided by bending the knee to the right height.

Keep a fair distance between the racket head and the ball for you to make good contact with the ball. Please remember a longer backswing helps a flatter shot.

If you want to topspin or roll the ball, make sure your arm is comfortably stretched out to the side of the body with a racket head closer to your head.

If you are using an open stance, you will hit the ball by facing your opponent. You can cover a lot of the court with this stance and hit those short crosscourt strokes that used to be my favourite.

You need to use a lot of your arm and shoulder power as you are not using your body weight. The idea is to keep your playing arm and shoulders relaxed and move the racket to a power position to stroke the ball. Hit the ball do not choke. To get a good topspin hit under the ball as it starts dropping.

Follow-through

A good follow-through and finish are essential to ensure the ball moves in the intended direction. During the contact point, you want the racket to be accelerating and not slowing down unless you are planning another shot like a lob or a drop. After the contact, you must finish using a complete follow-through, at the very end of the swing path.

A good finish will help to stretch the muscles and avoids jerks that lead to injury. You finish the follow through with the playing arm and elbow across the chest with a good bend in that joint. The racket head must finish above or in line with the opposite shoulder.

From a management perspective too, you will appreciate a good follow-through is essential for any given task that we undertake. Nine times out of ten any assignment we undertake and do not follow through either falls off the table or is riddled with holes. We must prepare for any eventuality with focus, eye on the issue, seeing the wood for the trees, get ready with all our ammunition to hit the problem without injuring ourselves and resolve it to its very end.

Flat forehand follow-through

Forehand Cross Court

This is a stroke that is hit early. You meet the ball early and aim it towards your opponent's forehand, that is both of you are right-handers. Again the classical left leg forward using your body weight body to meet the ball early. You have players using an open stance to execute this stroke albeit with more arm and shoulder power. The deeper you hit the better.

Forehand Short Cross Court

This is always executed with an open stance with the ball falling much closer to and across the net, again connected early. I have won several points with this stroke.

Forehand Down the line

This is a stroke that is hit late. You meet the ball late and aim it towards your opponents backhand, that is assuming both of you are right-handers. Again the classical left leg forward using your body weight body to meet the ball this time a bit late. Using the open stance will make you lose control of the direction of the ball. The deeper you hit the better.

Forehand Drop-shot

For this stroke, you have to feel the ball. A drop shot is when you hit the ball softly over the net and let it land as close as possible to the net. It's best to hit a drop shot when the opponent is standing behind the baseline or out of position. A good drop shot will land barely over the net, enough to stretch the opponent. Using the Continental grip, shorten your backswing meet the ball with an open racket face, swing your racket through a cupping motion under the ball and slice it softly over the net using your body weight. A slight underspin is highly effective. Use the drop shot selectively and don't overdo it. Be ready to run up as your opponent might reach the ball and return with another drop shot! Experiment with a drop shot as an approach shot, too.

A SINGLE-HANDED BACKHAND

"MY SERVE AND MY FOREHAND I PRETTY MUCH ALWAYS HAD, BUT MY BACKHAND WAS A MADE BACKHAND. I WORKED ON IT FOR YEARS."- IVAN LENDL

Y ou must have a backhand. Most self-taught players try to avoid this shot by converting a backhand to a forehand! Time to get brave and learn that backhand.

The Grip for a Singlehanded Backhand

I recommend the Western grip, or a Continental or whatever you are comfortable with if you want to topspin or roll the ball, which is a combination of a flat stroke and a topspin or a flat stroke.

The Torso Turn.

As soon as you see the ball leaving your opponent's racket, start your torso swing to the left and backwards if you are a right-hander. Do not let your eye leave the ball.

Place your right leg forward, (right-handers) pointing the right shoulder towards the ball and move to the ball sideways with the racket head higher than the wrist. The non-playing hand keeps supporting your racket while it is moving backwards. When you rotate your body, you are automatically coiling the oblique muscles. While rotating your shoulder you are already moving your racket head to a ready position with your backswing to hit the ball. This will stop you from waiting for the ball till the last second before beginning your backswing.

Getting ready to meet the ball.

Stroking the ball.

Drop your knees to the level of the ball. Then uncoil and swing in your shoulder, your hip with your body weight behind the ball for power. Do not reduce the speed of the swing, just go through the stroke transferring your weight to the forward leg, without choking the shot. It is ideal to have your knee almost in line with the ball, bending it to the height required. Many errors can be avoided by bending the knee to the right height.

Remember to keep your racket head higher than the wrist and then begin the swing uncoiling your upper body, and swing through transferring your weight to the forward leg.

Do not keep an open stance.

You need to use a lot of your arm and shoulder power as you are not using your body weight. The idea is to keep your playing arm and shoulders relaxed and move the racket to a power position to stroke the ball. Hit the ball do not choke.

The Follow Through

A good follow-through and finish are essential to ensure the ball moves in the intended direction. A poor follow-through can lead to injury and ruin all the effort so far. During the contact point, you want the racket to be accelerating and not slowing down unless you are planning another shot like a lob or a drop. After the contact, you must finish using a complete follow-through, at the very end of the swing path.

A good finish will help to stretch the muscles and avoids jerks that lead to injury, finishing with the playing hand elbow across the chest with a good bend in that joint. The racket head may finish above or in line with the opposite shoulder.

Flat backhand follow-through

The One-Handed Backhand Slice.

This stroke can be used as an aggressive shot to run up to the net or it can be used to keep the ball in play (rally), lob, skim the net, counter a topspin shot or drop shot as well.

The Grip for a Backhand Slice

I recommend the Western grip, or a Continental or whatever you are comfortable with if you want to topspin or roll the ball, which is a combination of a flat stroke and a topspin or a flat stroke.

It is the other way around if you are a left-hander. This is an important part as the non-stroking hand supports the racket weight, keeps the movement in the correct arc, and eases the tension on the playing hand.

The Torso Turn.

As soon as you see the ball leaving your opponent's racket, start your torso swing to the left and back-wards if you are a right-hander. Do not let your eye leave the ball.

Place your right leg forward, (right-handers) point-ing the right shoulder towards the ball and move to the ball sideways with the racket head higher than the wrist. The non-playing hand keeps supporting your racket while it is moving backwards. When you rotate your body, you are automatically coiling the oblique muscles. While rotating your shoulder you are already moving your racket head to a ready position with your backswing to hit the ball. This will stop you from waiting for the ball till the last second before beginning your backswing.

Your non-dominant hand should remain on the throat of the racquet and your hitting arm should be slightly bent at the elbow and the racquet's head higher than usual, at an angle to slice the ball with weight on your back foot.

Stroking the ball

You swing in transferring your weight from the back foot to the front foot. Your racket head is facing slightly towards you as you contact the ball. Here is when you feel the ball and move with the ball forward, you do not slack or fall back as you hit the ball. Your upper torso remains sideways. Your non-playing arm will automatically move in the opposite direction. . It is ideal to have your knee almost in line with the ball, bending it to the height required. Many errors can be avoided by bending the knee to the right height.

Follow-through

The follow-through is an important element of any stroke. It should be in the direction of where you want the ball to go. Keep the following in your mind.

- ☺ The racquet will stay across your body.
- ☺ The racquet head should be open and slightly towards you and high at the beginning of the swing.

☺ Remain sideways at contact.

☺ Feel the ball as you make contact and hit through, not down. Hitting down will make you lose speed, and the ball will drop closer to the net and the opponent will kill it.

☺ Do not let the ball go higher than your shoulder. Meet the ball early and on the rise.

☺ Do not drop your wrist. The racket head remains above the wrist level.

☺ Keep the ball low over the net.

A SERVE

"BUSINESS IS LIKE TENNIS. THOSE WHO SERVE WELL WIN."- KEN BLANCHARD

Your ultimate weapon is in tennis is your Serve. You have absolute control as you begin the point, and with excellent service, you can get the point as well. To take advantage of your body weight, avoid an open stance. You need to stand sidewise with your nonplaying arm shoulder pointing at the service box on the opponent's side.

The Grip

The grip you use to serve will dictate your entire swing.

Shake hands with your racket and then move your palm ever so lightly to the left (right-handers) and create a V with your thumb and forefinger. Place your hand on the racquet so that this V is at 11 o'clock, or one o'clock for left-handed players.

Hold your racquet as you would a hammer. This is called the Continental Grip explained earlier on.

Practice maintaining this grip while keeping your hand loose and relaxed.

Large numbers of club players tend to use an Eastern forehand grip to serve with, with the sole objective of somehow get the ball across. The second serve tends to become an apology of a serve.

When you try to use power for a flat or a spin with your eastern grip as you progress, you could face a lot of strain on your tendons and end up with an injury. If you use a forehand grip to serve with, you might be able to get lots of power because the grip allows you to hit the ball very flat, however, your consistency and accuracy will suffer greatly and generating spins will be very hard, if not impossible.

Most professional players use the continental grip to serve or use some sort of variation of it.

Visualize your serve.

By picturing a strong, successful service, you can help to decrease anxiety, thus lessen the likelihood of making mistakes. Take deep, calming breaths. Imagine the force of the service and the sound of the ball hitting the racquet. Visualize the whole process of your service from start to finish and the ball reaching the intended spot.

Hold the ball in your fingertips or the way you would hold a glass of water. By holding it like this, you can more accurately control the toss.

The ready position for a Serve.

You are standing sideways, with your non-throwing arm shoulder pointing in the direction of the opponent, for right-handers, the left foot at a 45-degree position and the back foot nearly parallel to the baseline. The heel of the forward foot is aligned to the toe of the rear foot. And take a deep breath and breathe out. This is very important. It will calm you down for the perfect serve.

You are ready with your continental grip, do not get into the Eastern grip. Your weight is on the back foot.

Bounce the ball with your hands only, do not use

your racket to bounce the ball. You have frozen at the point you are and breathing evenly.

Throw the ball before transferring your body weight from your back foot to the front foot.

You are now ready to strike the ball, hitting elbow bent, racket head pointing up towards the sky.

Your non-hitting hand pointing towards the ball, tracking it. The right shoulder dropped back and down with a good knee bend, ready to launch the body off the ground.

Your head is looking up towards your target - the ball.

Tossing the Ball

This should be done by raising the arm straight and releasing the ball from your fingertips when your arm is about head height. You should be tossing the ball a bit higher than the place you want to make contact.

Keep your eyes on the ball. An easy way to do this is by keeping your tossing arm raised during the serve. If you allow your arm to drop, you will drop your head as well. Stay relaxed and focused on the service, rather than glancing at your opponent or the net. It's imperative to keep your eye on the ball with your eyes all the time!

Transfer your weight to your back foot. As your shift, your weight to your back foot, lift the ball off your front foot.

This is yet another part that will dictate not only your swing, but also the direction, and the power. Lots of players get it wrong, and there is no need to if you follow a simple example. Draw a 1 ft semicircle around your foot, like the size of your foot with shoes on, stand sideways with your left shoulder facing the direction you want the ball to go, toss the ball, with your elbow straight, and let it drop. It should drop within the semi-circle. Do those 100 times every day.

Once you master this, the rest is easy. All you need to do is to toss the ball slightly to the right for a slice and slightly behind and to the left along with a change in the foot positions to get topspin. More later this subject.

The next part of your toss is equally important. With your elbow straight, the ball should travel up to the maximum point you can reach with your racket face, on your toes.

Tossing the ball way too high will cause a break in the momentum on your service motion and you will end up halfway in your swing waiting for the ball to drop to a convenient point for you to hit. This will also cause the ball to go all over the place, especially in the wind. So, have a consistent and steady tossing arm with an up and down motion with your elbow straight and aim to your contact point as explained or at the most six inches above the contact point. Hold the ball in your fingers like you are holding a glass of water and not in the palm of your hand and release the ball when the hand reaches head height.

Toss for the First Serve:

Practice gently tossing the ball forward and farther into the court. This will add your bodyweight to the Serve as you lean in and run up to the net.

Toss for the Second Serve: Roll

The same principle, just adds a bit more roll (frontal spin not topspin) by hitting the ball on its 2 'o 'clock position. Use your wrist to get that roll. Tossing the ball too much behind you will make you lose power, and the opponent will kill it.

Toss for the Second Serve: Slice

Toss the ball slightly to the right, farther out from the body and hit the ball at an angle, bringing the ball into the court.

Contact with the ball

Moving your back foot or right leg (right-handers) swing the racquet arm up and over your opposite shoulder. Your racket arm should begin in a curved position behind you as you prepare to serve. As the tossed ball starts to drop, swing your racquet arm up to contact the ball. Your arm should be completely extended when it meets the ball. You are not aiming to create any sort of spin, you are simply trying to hit the back of the ball, bang on with the centre of your racket.

Pronation and Supination

I recommend you try this after you learn to hit flat and a slice Serve.

When you turn your palm upwards towards the sky, your forearm and hand are supinated. If you turn your palm downwards, towards the ground, you are pronating your palm and forearm fully. Most strong servers use the principle of supination and pronation during their service motions.

The higher the supination before contact, the more you can "wrist-snap" your racket through the contact zone using pronation.

Some players will use very little supination before contact and then go straight through with pronation, however, Pete Sampras used a great deal of supination on serve to generate more "whip" through the contact point.

Remember you are largely using your forearm for pronating; the wrist comes into play for the kick.

The Finish

One of the main causes of serve breakdown or even worse, injury, is an incorrect finish or follow through. When you hit your serve, your body should be in a relaxed state and the follow-through should be relaxed and allow the arm and body to slow down in a natural way using the correct muscle groups. If during the high-speed swing we suddenly stop altogether or finish in the wrong way, you will injure the shoulder, elbow and wrist. If this is done time and time again, the result can be a serious injury. A natural, relaxed follow-through should take the racket to the left hip, a great way to remember this finish is to imagine your racket is a gun and you are placing it back into a holster. The elbow should be bent when you are finishing to take the stress off your shoulder joint, a straight arm places a great deal of stress there.

Types of Serves

We always start with a flat serve. Then move on to the slice and then on to rolling the ball or a high kick topspin serve.

The Flat serve

For a typical flat serve, you would want to hit the ball flat on the string bed to gain the most amount of power from pronation. The fastest, and possibly the most intimidating, is the flat serve, where you are using the combination of your body weight, your shoulder and your arm. Barry MacKay the American tennis player was perhaps one of the first players to serve flat and fast. It was most effective on the lawn courts. To be effective, the flat serve must be precise and perfectly executed.

The Slice Serve

The Slice Serve is one of the most effective ways to start a point on serve when you want to control the direction of the ball. If executed correctly, a good slice serve will open the court for you to hit your next shot. Always plan your next shot after the current one. It can also be used as a good second serve.

The key to imparting a decent slice that will also spin the ball is the angle of the racket face at contact.

For a slice serve however we want to hit the ball on roughly 2 o clock side of the ball which will give you the power and get the ball to dip down as well after the bounce.

Visualize your service from the start to the finish including the ball touching the target point, taking a deep breath, let go.

Follow-through

As with all the strokes, follow-through plays an important part. Make sure that, after hitting the ball, you continue to swing through until the racquet is at your opposite hip bringing your racquet down across your body. If you choke or drop the speed, the service will not have its full force.

Back to the ready position

Then get back to the ready position by transferring your weight evenly over both feet.

A VOLLEY

"IF YOU DIDN'T HAVE POWER, YOU HAD TO HAVE TOUCH AND SERVE AND VOLLEY, WHICH I FOUND VERY EXCITING AND THAT'S WHY I LOVE WATCHING FEDERER PLAY, BECAUSE OF THOSE SKILLS."- EVONNE GOOLAGONG CAWLEY

A volley is a shot that you return before the ball bounces. We perform our volleys at the service line or closer to the net. Volleying from the service line is a tad risky as there is a danger of slipping into the 'No man's land' that is between the service line and the baseline. Another risk is that you can get passed easier if you hang around the service line too long. Volleys are usually aggressive because their primary function is to make your opponent move faster or interrupt the timing of the rally, giving you a chance to catch them off guard or instantly hit a winner. The backhand volley requires the support of the non-playing hand. The volley continues to be my favourite stroke. As I had started playing on lawns I had got into the habit of was serving and running up to the net. A lot of advantages in going up to the net, firstly the net is a lot closer, so lesser chances of hitting the ball into the net. Standing at the net gives me better control over the court. Plus it saves me the bother of running side to side on the baseline.

When you're at the net, every second counts, and to

stay up on the net you need to get the volleying technique right and master your smashes, as only two things can happen, either you get passed or you get lobbed. The closer you are to the net, the less space the opponent has to pass you. I look for every opportunity to run up to the net as I am confident with my volleys.

The Grip for Volleys

Most players use a Continental grip for volleys, though some advanced players may use an Eastern forehand grip for their forehand volleys. My recommendation is to use the Continental grip as it is most efficient for hitting both forehand and backhand volleys without changing your grip.

The ready position.

The ready position for a volley is the same as explained, just that you need to be quicker as the ball is going to approach much faster.

The Forehand volley: Punch the ball

There is no time for a backswing unless it is a loose shot coming your way. I can still hear my coach yell "punch the ball, don't hit it, punch it". It took me a while to understand what he meant.

Ideally, as you see the ball leaving your opponent's

racket face, right-handers move the racket face just in line with the shoulder, (Punch volleys require no backswing) with an open stance, coiling your upper torso, then move in with your left leg forward moving your body weight forward to meet the ball.

You come in with a slightly open racket face and punch the ball with your racket face in a downward cut in the motion. Move your hand in the direction that you want the ball to go and keep your head down and your eye on the ball.

It is ideal to have your knee is almost in line with the ball, bending it to the height required. Many errors can be avoided by bending the knee to the right height.

The Backhand volley: Punch the ball

As in the forehand, backhand punch volleys require no backswing. You coil your upper torso to the left (right-handers) then move in with your right leg forward moving your body weight forward to meet the ball. It is ideal to have your knee almost in line with the ball, bending it to the height required. Many errors can be avoided by bending the knee to the right height.

You come in with a slightly open racquet face and punch the ball with your racket face in a downward cut in the motion. Move your hand in the direction that you want the ball to go and keep your head down and your eye on the ball.

The Drop Volley

An ideal shot when your opponent is on the baseline. A drop volley is a drop shot you perform while at the net. It is a low volley with a light touch placed close to the net, furthest away from the opponent. You need to feel the ball and the best drop volley will tire your opponent and break his rhythm.

Feel the ball for a drop volley.

Block Volley

This will happen when you are caught unawares, or the opponent is too close to you when you can barely move. This is when you just have enough time to block the ball and put it away if you can.

Lob Volley

This happens when two players approach the net simultaneously, or you have reached the net and the opponent is coming in. Instead of trying to pass, or get into in-court volleys, you can perform a lob, which involves opening up the racket face and giving the ball a high arc over your opponent's head that is far enough to pass them, but closer to the baseline.

The Half Volley

A half volley is hit off the ground right as the ball is on the rise just after bouncing. The timing is even more difficult than a regular volley because you're hitting the ball after the bounce, not before. While the half volley isn't a true volley, it still requires a similar compact movement and quick footwork and comes in handy when you are running up to the net. The basic points to remember is to bend your knees, racket head above the wrist and eye on the ball. At 69, this shot is useful for me as I can't get to the net fast enough after my serve.

A LOB

"OFTEN CALLED UPON AND RARELY PRACTISED" ROD LAVER.

You need to practice this shot or you could give your opponent an advantage over you. This is a shot that goes over the opponent's head and forces him to run back and return after the after drop. A not too effective lob can be smashed. A lob can be used as an aggressive or defective tactic. It is a powerful weapon in your arsenal. No one likes lobbers. They can make your life miserable by forcing you to smash. Then a lob can throw a person completely out of rhythm. Recreational players often get scared of being lobbed in tennis matches so they tend to stay just inside the service line, which helps them to reach the lobs easier. The preferred grip is Continental.

An Aggressive Lob

An aggressive lob can be a topspin that is executed when opponents are at the net and you move up to the net provided are sure your lob cannot be smashed. A lob can also be sliced above the opponent's head, again as you move up to the net. Try sending the ball over the opponent's backhand deep into the corner with an open racket face. You can try it when the sun is on your opponent's face.

A Defensive Lob

This is to be used when you are totally out of position and you have no recourse but to lob, preferably over your opponent's head. Even if your lob is not effective, you still get time to resume your ready position to meet and return the smash.

Note the open racket face for the lob.

AN OVERHEAD SMASH

"FINISH YOUR OPPONENT WITH AN OVERHEAD SMASH"

A smash is easier said than done. A seemingly easy smash can be flubbed if you go awry with your timing. This is a shot where your timing has to be perfect. The eye is always on the ball after you see where your opponents are standing. Normally they would be waiting to meet the ball well behind the baseline. An effective smash bounces near the baseline and goes well over the player's head.

If you serve and volley or attack the net like me, chances are your opponent will throw up lobs to force you back or discourage you from coming up to the net too often.

Get Sideways

The first thing to do is to get sideways by pivoting back with your right leg (left leg for left-handers) and turn your shoulders so that your left shoulder is facing towards the net. This ensures that you have a full upper torso and hip turn and can generate rotational power on your overhead smash when you hit the ball. While you are turning your body sideways, you will need to start your backswing by lifting the racket head to your right side around head height whilst also lifting your non-hitting hand, towards the oncoming ball while coiling your body.

The Contact

You are now more or less reaching your trophy position like on the Serve. On the overhead smash, we have less time to have a big swing because the ball will dip in quickly especially if the opponent has hit a topspin lob. As we have less time on the overhead smash, keep the swing more compact and ensure we hit the ball out in front of our heads. You can use your non-hitting arm to track the ball to help you judge the distance and contact the ball on time. You can point your index finger at the ball to help you keep track.

Footwork

This is the right time to get yourself into the position into the correct position with your feet. This means that you use the correct footwork patterns to move back behind the ball (See the practice sessions section of this book) and then move forward if you have time if you feel the ball is going to land ahead of you. It's always a better idea to beat the ball by going back first and then move forward, rather than the opposite, like moving forward firstly and then having to rush back to cover a deep lob. If the lob is not too deep you can use the normal side shuffle. This is ideal when you only have to move three or four steps. Then make contact out in front of your body extending up for maximum power, also transferring your body weight into the shot.

MENTAL ASPECT OF THE GAME

"TENNIS IS MOSTLY MENTAL. YOU WIN OR LOSE THE MATCH BEFORE YOU EVEN GET OUT THERE." - SERENA WILLIAMS

Four years back I was on the tennis court with my mates with deteriorating footwork and questionable fitness level, although not too bad for 65 years of a fairly fast-paced lifestyle. We started a match after warming up. While at the far end of my forehand corner I anticipated a drop-shot floating to my backhand (I am a right-hander). Desperate to reach the ball, I couldn't stop and went straight into the net, head over heels.

Pressure is part of the game at any age and any level especially when you are trained to value every point. The mental aspect is a performance-determining factor in tennis. Players understand that variations in focus, intensity and emotional state however small have a great impact on performance. Our experience says that every time we go on the court to play a game, we cannot expect to execute shots that we normally hit perfectly well during practice.

Anxiety, fear, tension and disappointment are just a few of the negativities that accompanies us on-court, that which sport psychologists are working hard to remove through different techniques. Everyone is trying to teach how to overcome negativity and operate in an optimal state of mind that would allow us to play at our highest potential.

One major factor here is capability. It is important to understand that if you possess a technically ineffective serve, no amount of visualization, relaxation or thought control will help. You must use the correct grip, a relaxed swing, power, rhythm or anything else that will allow you to operate at your highest potential. Mental toughness will only allow you to hit your deficient serve at the best level your technique allows. My objective for this chapter and the book is to provide you with the gift of positivity: to help you understand what your true capability is and then perform reliably from that space.

Tennis is unique, mentally demanding and an individual sport, which is more stressful than a team event because the sport is all about "you." Each player must confront the situation.

No Coaching is allowed during a match. You are alone (singles) while you are playing in a tournament or a friendly match with your mates. The friendliness vanishes the second practice is over!

The players call whether the shots are in or out,

except for the quarter-finals, semi and finals, as matches are played without a referee in most tournaments during the initial rounds. Each player calls the lines on his side. In other words, you are at the mercy of your opponent's ethical values. I was faced with a dreadful experience when my opponent decided to walk up to the net to shake my hand assuming the match was over according to his score-keeping!

Tennis is not arguably the fastest sport. There is a lot of time to think in between points and during changeovers. The sport is a mix of being fully engaged and preparing to play. One is in and out of the 'focused playing zone'.

The game is not over until you win the last point. That requires players to maintain their focus, intensity and concentration from the first point to the last one, with the constant pressure of a potential comeback by the opponent.

A breakpoint creates unnecessary anxiety.

Every time you are on the court you are not only battling the opponent but also the changing conditions of wind, sun, different surfaces, indoor or outdoor courts. Players must adapt.

We need to understand and accept that losing is an integral part of existence.

Your ability awareness

Become aware of your ability level. Awareness about what you can and cannot do on the court will help you reach a mental state that will allow you to perform up to your potential. You need a balance between power and control using constructive practice sessions and plenty of match play. Ask yourself, are you missing because you are anxious? Are you simply hitting the wrong shot? Is the shot in the right direction at a speed you cannot control? Only after you understand what you should be doing on the court, and if your mistakes are truly affected by the mental state of your mind, will a psychological approach succeed.

Let us delve into the mind to learn how to create the ideal mental state to allow you to play up to your potential consistently. Make your peace with anxiety. Many players believe that as their skill level improve, they will be less pressured when competing. The reality is that as your performance increases so does your opponents'. You do tend to be nervous as a beginner because you are not sure if you can place the second serve in, so you serve a weak pop for the opponent to kill. Playing as a seeded player in a tournament, you are anxious because if you do not secure the second service at a good speed and close to the line you will certainly lose the point. Accept pressure, if winning or losing matters to you. Many players view pressure as a weakness, which makes things worse. The minute you accept that being apprehensive is normal, working on strategies to overcome becomes easier. The thought process is not about eliminating but accepting pressure as part of the game.

You are anxious when you doubt your ability to win a match that you think you should win. Here is an incident to muse upon. I met a person who was fond of lobbing. He fetched up as my opponent in the first round in a tournament where I was seeded #1. He had spread the word that he would beat me as he knew of my weakness and made sure his words reached my ears. Sure, enough his words were playing out in my subconscious, and then this joker started lobbing every single shot throwing my rhythm totally out of gear. After losing a game in the set, I sat down to introspect and decide my strategy. I reminded myself that I was better in every way and had no business to get rattled. I went on to win 6-1, 6-0.

You play someone much better than you and with absolutely no chance of winning, you can play without pressure giving your best shot. I lost to Ion Tiriac in the Asians and Alex Metreveli while trying impossible shots as I had nothing to lose. Again, if you play someone not up to your standards, with no chance of beating you, pressure is not going to be a factor, unless someone applies psychological pressure. Pressure arrives when you know things can go either way and you need to win.

Once you do not care about winning or losing, you will not be stressed. The level of pressure is completely dependent on your assessment of the situation. One suggestion is to change your perspective. Accept that everything is relative in life and based on your chosen point of view.

We moved from a large house abroad to a smaller apartment in India. We were uncomfortable initially, then once we accepted the situation, we realised the apartment with a support system seems just about right now that we are 69 and 65. The same happens in any situation. Whenever we chose to view a situation as a threat, pressure will immediately rear its ugly head. On the other hand, if you view the same situation as a challenge, the feelings that you will elicit will be different. I was the Business Head of a company whose Balance Sheet reflected a hopeless situation. I accepted the challenge and with a bit of luck turned the company around.

Couple of things you can try when you are on the court.

Believe that tennis not only improves your level of fitness and fun but also provides you with the tremendous opportunity to practice solving problems under pressure. Go from winning to enjoying and performing. Do not focus on the result and its consequences.

Drop your ego and don't bother about what others think of your game.

Focus on what you need to do in the next point to give yourself the best chance of winning the point and keep doing this point after point. Shift your focus from the possible result of the point to the task at hand.

Performance goals direct you towards playing in a certain way. Say to yourself "I want to hit the ball early and run up to the net on every short ball". "I will hit my topspin backhand every time I am in the right position". "I will stroke the ball when it is on the rise and be more aggressive when returning second serves". Instead of saying to yourself 'do not double fault', say exactly what you can do to improve your chances against double-faulting. Go through the motions of the Serve in your mind with the outcome you desire.

Be in the present moment. The "Present moment" in Tennis makes total sense and that is to perform at your best you need to focus solely on that particular stroke and stay away from any other distracting thought.

Once the ball is in play, the ball becomes your world, and your job is to follow that ball like a hawk chasing its prey. I like to use the analogy of a tennis match or practise being like a meditation, with the ball taking the place of the breath or mantra. That sounds quite easy, right? Just keep your eye on the ball! I find controlling my thoughts much harder than controlling the ball.

The Magic mantra is to KEEP YOUR EYE ON THE BLESSED BALL. You need to practice. The ball is your universe. My coach used to constantly yell "The ball should look like a football to you". The penny finally dropped, and I got the message. I started to "eye" the ball for while and would not think of anything else during the game.

WHAT SHOULD YOU DO BETWEEN POINTS?

P repare yourself to perform at your best during the next point.

Here are three things that you need to accomplish between the end of a point and the start of the next one:

1) Make sure you mentally move on from the last one if it was regrettable. If you need extra time after blowing an easy shot or after a very long rally, do what the pros do: Take extra time, go to your towel and calm down. Looking at your racket strings is a good way to avoid distractions. Once you are back in control physically and emotionally move on.

2) Plan the next point. You need to be clear about how you want to play the next point.

3) Plan your strategy, you should consider things like should you attack or be consistent? Should you play to your opponent's weakness or surprise him by changing your normal pattern, or mix up pace and height? How are you going to start the point? What

kind of Serves are you going to hit? Where are you going to serve? Are you serving and volleying? Attack a weak return and run up to the net?

In my experience, planning more than two shots with a clear idea of how you want to start the point and what type of point you would like to play goes a long way towards improving your performance.

Final Checklist

Make sure that your mind and body are ready to play the next point. Using the time wisely between points will guarantee that you play each point to the best of your ability so be diligent about it.

WHAT SHOULD YOU DO BETWEEN GAMES DURING CHANGEOVERS?

The changeovers are a time for recovery, analysis and tactical preparation. Use the time to drink, eat something light (A banana is a great energy giver) and relax while at the same time analyzing what is happening in the match.

Ask yourself "How am I winning the points"? "How am I losing the points"? "Where does he like to hit"? "Where is his or her weak area, what kind of shots is he or she missing"?

By answering these questions, you should establish a tactical plan. Keep it simple. Focus on one or two things that you would like to try and stay flexible as the match progresses, changing the course as needed.

EMOTIONAL CONTROL.

"IF YOU WANT TO BE A CHAMPION, YOU HAVE GOT TO FEEL LIKE ONE, YOU HAVE GOT TO ACT LIKE ONE, YOU HAVE TO LOOK LIKE ONE."-RED AUERBACH

Live in the present moment

Do not let your mind digress to things other than the job at hand, enjoying tennis. It will take you precisely 60 seconds to feel miserable. Just think of yourself, your regrets of the past and the anxiety of the future. Instead, condition your mind to live in the moment. Make it a habit to be happy, no matter what the situation is.

Manipulate your mind

You can learn to manipulate your state of mind. If you want to change your emotions, you can do it by changing your thoughts, by changing your body language or by doing both. Try smiling, more often, and you will see what I mean.

Focus

There are no such things as good or bad thoughts. There are only thoughts that help your performance and thoughts that hinder it, so your job as a competitor is to constantly focus your attention on those ideas that support your performance. The same applies to your work front. The idea is to win a few more points than your opponent. That is usually the difference between winning and losing.

Think one point at a time

During the game or a match or a tournament, the objective is to do everything possible to improve your chances of winning each of the points played – one point at a time. The thoughts about winning or losing, the way you are playing, other irrelevant issues often leads to more mistakes. Focusing only on the current moment gets easier when you are playing a game.

During a match, your inner dialogue sets the tone of your performance. You are your coach, and you need to take that role seriously. Work hard on being the best coach that you can be. Make sure that everything you tell yourself is helping your performance. Give yourself unambiguous directions that you can easily follow.

Avoid useless internal dialogues

"Hit the ball in, do not double fault or win this point" are useless instructions because they are too vague.

RITUALS

"I THINK WHEN YOU COM-
PETE EVERY WEEK WHEN
YOU PLAY UNDER PRESSURE
DAILY, YOU FIND YOUR RIT-
UALS TO BE 100 PER CENT,
FOCUSED ON WHAT YOU
ARE DOING"- RAFAEL NADAL

I get into my zone as soon as I have wished my opponent in the dressing room.

I would have completed my visualization process by then and would walk onto the court without looking at the gallery, wished the umpire if there was one, (as during the initial rounds the players would keep the points).

I would keep my bag, take out my rackets, choose the one on the spot, take the balls and bounce them with the face of my racket all the way while walking to the baseline, keep bouncing the ball, my eyes only on the ball. I would be keenly aware of the smell from the ball, the court.

Once I knew my opponent has reached the other side I would start the rallying. Stroking the ball at my opponent and keeping the ball in play. All the while I would notice the shots that my opponent was hitting, backhands and forehands, and run-up to the net to start volleying, being my core strength area. I would request him to toss a couple of balls in the air for me to practice my overhead. Everything that I did on the court had a purpose. While volleying I would notice his footwork. I would notice whether he was bending his knee, gather his weaknesses, when he lobbed, put him under pressure by smashing consistently. I would not hit a single winner during practice. I would come back to the planet as soon as the start of the toss was announced. An then get back into my zone again.

Rituals are distinct personal tasks that help you focus. They are especially useful for handling pressure situations. You have things like bouncing the ball before serving, rub your hand on your shorts, or stretching, whatever without being obnoxious.

A good warm-up ritual will make sure you step on the court ready to play your best from the first point. It should include a total body warm-up routine composed of stretching, jogging, running and jumping exercises that render the body ready to work at 100% intensity.

Use the time to visualize and plan your match. Rehearse your performance exactly the way you want to play, including your tactical goals. Focus on the mental part of your ritual. Are your thoughts helping you to start the point with energy and confidence? Don't say "Please don't double fault" or "You are a moron" as it does more damage to your psyche.

GIVE YOURSELF POSITIVE MESSAGES

"**A**im high over the net, keep your racket head up, watch the ball, attack the net on the first short ball" are much better.

Choose phrases and ideas to build yourself up and not to tear yourself down. Phrases like "You are an xxx! You will never win" are not solid building blocks. They are more like sinking stones that will quickly drown you.

Find statements that work well for you. Everyone is different.

Keep a count of negative thoughts when you play next. You don't need to discuss it. Just remember it next time you fall into the pit. Slowly you will get over it.

Understanding the problem is winning half the battle. The next step is to work on replacing those negative thoughts. Start thinking of better alternatives each time you have a negative thought. It takes a while to change the habit, I should know but consciously replacing your negative thoughts with better alternatives will slowly transform your self-coaching into a truly empowering tool.

BODY LANGUAGE

"I SEE TENDENCIES, I SEE BODY LANGUAGE"- MICHAEL CHANG

Body language is a reflection of your emotions, and emotions are a reflection of your body language. Feeling powerful, secure, and self-assured requires body language reflecting those emotions, which will help you to develop a presence on the court that conveys these emotions. I used to hear had great body language, no one could determine whether I was winning or losing by looking at me. Regardless of the score, your gestures and body language should exude confidence and send a clear message to your opponent: I am coming for you, every single point!

Fake it till you make it

You must have heard about "Fake it till you make it." The way we see ourselves is nothing but a story that we have chosen to believe. Most of the time when things are going badly, we have no problem berating ourselves, yet, we are hesitant to accept what we have done well. We are so easy to believe negativity and ever so doubtful about positivity. If you hit a good shot it is a fluke and if you hit a bad shot it is a bad shot!

VISUALIZATION

"EXERCISE AND SPORTS ARE GREATLY AFFECTED BY WHAT GOES INTO THE MIND, AND THE MIND IS GREATLY AFFECTED BY SPORTS AND EXERCISE AS WELL. THIS IS TRUE AMONG EXERCISERS AT ALL LEVELS, DESPITE THEIR DIFFERENT GOALS. A MAJOR ELEMENT IN MENTAL TRAINING IS VISUALIZATION ... VISUALIZING A POSITIVE OUTCOME CAN CREATE A PATTERN OF SUCCESS, AS LONG AS YOU SET REALISTIC AND SPECIFIC GOALS."— GRETE WAITZ

I have spoken about it earlier visualizing your Serve till its conclusion. Lots of books have been written on the subject. Unfortunately, it is easier said than done. Vividly imagining yourself serving with a perfect motion and absolute confidence is not easy when you are a champion of double- faults at crucial moments.

The traditional way to practice visualization involves:

Close your eyes and imagine yourself playing.

Focus on taking slow and deep breaths and tell yourself to relax deeper and deeper.

Think of a point right before serving or returning or before executing a new stroke.

Form an ideal picture in your head of what you want to accomplish.

The picture has to be as real as possible. You need to involve as many senses as you can. Think of colours, smells, feelings, emotions and sounds.

Play with the image. Change angles, distances and

perspectives. Remember, the better your mental story the more effective it will be.

To finish the exercise, slowly change your focus, open your eyes and feel rested and confident. Period.

Another method to deploy would be shadowing, imagine a perfect execution while shadowing the stroke you want to improve. Shadowing on the court or in front of a mirror, or visualizing as I watched someone perfectly executing the stroke I wanted to improve, made a substantial difference. Find out what works best for you!

MUSCLE MEMORY

Although skills, like cycling or perfecting a tennis serve, might require the strengthening of certain muscles, the processes that are important for learning and memory of new skills occur mainly in the brain.

Recall the time when you learnt to ride a bicycle when younger. Did you learn to ride your bicycle by reading a book about it or practice riding the bike? With repetition, you retained a motor image of the procedure. That made it easy for to be able to get on a bicycle and ride with relative ease.

Although skills, like cycling or perfecting a tennis serve, might require the strengthening of certain muscles, the processes that are important for learning and memory of new skills occur mainly in the brain. Muscle memories stored in your brain are much like a cache of frequently enacted tasks for your muscles.

Our muscles remember information or procedures that were practised many times. Muscle memory is a powerful learning tool!

Repetition of the correct technique is the only answer as it addresses muscle memory. It is alike repeating positive thoughts throughout the day till it becomes a habit, your brain being a muscle. Playing a musical instrument is yet another example wherein constant repeating of a pattern of strokes gets ingrained in your muscle memory. Think of moments after you have hit a great shot or your best wins. The positive feeling after cracking a good deal. The feeling of success as you cross your bottom-line projections. Think of those moments repeatedly so that positivity gets ingrained into your muscle memory.

Ingrained faulty technique

Changes that occur in the brain during skill learning and memory alter the information that the brain sends out to the muscles, thereby changing the movements that are produced.

So It does take a while to get over the faulty technique developed for many years. It is difficult to erase the muscle memory. The opposite is true as well. A proper technique ingrained in your body will always remain an asset for you.

It takes hours of repetition, to break down the negativity resulting from years of hesitation, fear and lack of confidence. After a while, these feelings and actions become a habit, and you no longer realize they are there.

Practice, Practice and Practice that is the only way out. Playing a game is not practice.

THE PRACTICE SESSIONS.

"CHAMPIONS KEEP PLAYING UNTIL THEY GET IT RIGHT"- BILLY JEAN KING

Rally

Practising to keep the ball in play is one of the most important aspects of tennis that combines focus, relaxation and competition.

Why: This session will help you gain control of the ball, of yourself and your mind.

When: Preferably every day or decide on a day when you can dedicate 20 minutes for this exercise only.

What: The objective is to simply keep the ball in play.

How: This exercise can be done at a pace that is comfortable for both players and can be very slow too. The farther you are from the net, the higher you need to hit, the closer you are lower you need to target. The racket face decides the height the ball will fly. Higher the ball, lower the speed and vice versa. Return the ball to your opponent at a point where he can return with the least amount of movement. After every shot come back to the centre of the court and get into the ready position. Keep a count of your rallies and try to improve.

Forehand

This practice is to be split between 'down the line' and 'crosscourt', devoting 15 minutes for each, that's 30 minutes total towards the practice session. Assuming you and your opponent are right-handers when you hit a forehand down the line, your opponent returns with a backhand down the line. Again when you hit a forehand crosscourt your opponent gets to practice his Forehand crosscourt too.

Lob

Remember Rod Lavers words "Often called upon and rarely practised".

Devote 20 minutes towards practising your lob while your opponent practices his overhead smash. Practice sending your lob towards your opponent's backhand. You can start with simple flat overheads and as you gain control you can try rolling the ball. Similarly, on the backhand toss the ball over your opponents' backhand. Returning a lob on your backhand side is one of the more difficult shots.

Backhand

This practice is to be split between 'down the line' and 'crosscourt', devoting 15 minutes for each, that's 30 minutes total towards the practice session. Assuming you and your opponent are right-handers when you hit a backhand down the line, your opponent returns with a forehand down the line. Again when you hit a forehand crosscourt your opponent gets to practice his backhand crosscourt too.

Overhead Smash

This is the time when one of you will be tossing the ball up to the other person who will practice his overhead smash. You can try recovering, but I suggest keeping twenty-five practice balls in your bag and tossing them one after the other to your opponent. Devote 20mins for each person.

Volley

There are two methods to practice volleys.

In-court volleys

This can be practised as doubles or singles. Both players stand on either side of the court near the service line and punch the ball at each other. The ball has to be contacted, felt sideways on both sides, keep passing the ball to each other for the first couple of minutes forehand to forehand then switch to backhand to backhand and then on both sides. Total practice session 20 minutes. With two players on either side pass the ball to each player turn by turn.

Players take turns at the net. The one on the baseline should keep hitting the ball to the player on the net and get back to the ready position. The player at the net should volley the ball back to the player on the baseline and get back to the ready position at the net. Do this for both sides. Total practice session 20 minutes. With two players on either side pass the ball to each player turn by turn.

Remember to keep the racket head above the wrist, your eye is on the ball and 'punch' the ball sideways, not with an open stance.

Service

A Service can be practised on your own.

Keep 20 balls in the bag.

Start from the left side (backhand side for right-handers) of the court as this will give you more angles and will stretch your body especially the upper torso.

Keep a tennis ball box or a can on the opposite side of the court in each corner within the service box.

Out of the 20 balls in your bag take out 10 and aim for the backhand corner target. Then take out the balance 10 balls and aim for the other corner. The objective is to get your ball in with consistency and accuracy.

Now do the same exercise from the forehand side.

Once you are done you can walk over to the other side, collect the balls and resume your practice.

The same exercise can be done with another player who can practice service returns while the other Serves. The same exercise can be done foursome too.

You will surprise your mates!

Play points instead of a game

Replace a game with points and see the difference. You will have less pressure, will automatically relax and play better but still with a competitive edge.

☺ Let each player play 10 points from either side.

☺ Player 1 starts serving from the forehand side as usual but will be allowed only 1 serve.

☺ He serves 10 points and the ball goes over to the other side.

TENNIS ETIQUETTES

T his is a subject close to my heart. Etiquettes on and off the court were ingrained in us as young tennis players. I sure hope it is being taught today as well. It is like saying a 'thank you or please'. It is like waiting for somebody to finish speaking before you speak. Social etiquette is used in the tennis arena as well.

There are also some important unwritten laws under tennis etiquette. Tennis is a social game, a game involving simple politeness and consideration. Everyone will enjoy the game so much more if those standards are maintained.

☺ Always treat your opponents with courtesy and respect.

☺ Wait for the players to finish a point before crossing the court, even if they are practising.

☺ Always cross the court from behind the baseline, never in front of the players on the court, never while a point is in play. Wait until the point is over and then cross as fast as possible.

☺ Speak quietly when there are players on the court.

☺ If players are already on your court before you arrive, do not disturb them.

☺ Holding a court for another player is not permitted.

☺ Never ask players on the court when they are going to finish. Instead, ask the score politely.

☺ If a game has been announced by the players on the court, wait politely for them to finish.

☺ Do not switch players in the middle of a game without unanimous consent.

☺ Always warm-up (Stretching) well away from the court.

☺ If people are waiting, use the minimal time for knocking.

☺ You can call a point on your side, the opponent on the other side must accept it. If you are in doubt, the benefit goes to the opponent.

☺ If a ball lands on a neighbour's court, wait for an appropriate moment to retrieve it.

☺ If you are returning your neighbours ball, roll them onto the back of the court. Never send them back while a play is in progress. Do not pass the ball when the game is in play.

☺ The rule applies when you are playing,

☺ If a game is interrupted in any way, play the point again.

☺ It is the Server's responsibility to call out the

score if you are playing without an umpire.

☺ Do your best to keep from being abusive and yelling on the court.

☺ Never be aggressive with a ball picker.

☺ If you have spectators, do not let them get involved in line calling.

☺ If you have booked a court, be on time, and if you or your mates are late, allow the players waiting to start up.

☺ Do remember to thank the players who have let you have the court.

☺ You must thank your partner and your opponents after a game.

☺ Do not conduct loud postmortems of a point while in play. By all means, do it after the game.

☺ Bring balls, towels and water to drink.

☺ Wear appropriate gear including proper tennis shoes.

☺ Put away racket covers, ball cans, jackets etc., out of everyone's way, when you get on to the court.

☺ Retrieve balls for your partner and your opponent.

☺ Compliment your opponents on their good shots.

☺ Never throw the ball back to the server hard, instead politely return it after the point is played.

☺   Throw all the used cans, tin covers, edible left-overs, banana peels in the bin only.

COMMENTS & RESPONSES

Here are a few comments from recreational players. My responses are in italics.

"I played for 3 yrs from 2010 to 2014. Hadn't learnt the right way while I started and they just taught me to send back the ball somehow to the other side. Even the grip I have now is incorrect."

Congratulations on learning to hit the ball across the net on your own. Pat yourself on the back for being tenacious. Top players in the world have modified traditional grips over the years. The chapter on Grips will walk you through.

"Somehow I was able to return balls in a faster way. So opponents had difficulty in returning which I thought is a good way of playing."

If you can hit the ball hard and get it into the court,

that's a start. However, consistency matters. I would rather you slow down, keep the ball in play and reduce the number of unforced errors.

"After starting tennis in 2019 Oct only I started doing top spins, learnt backhand a bit. I get aggressive and hit the balls fast, all the balls am trying to hit to the opposite corner, is a topspin. I never play slow or drop. Also, my reflex is less and my leg doesn't move fast enough."

I am glad you restarted tennis after a break of four years. That shows your love for the game and your belief that it does help you in some way. Topspin is a good stroke as to hit a proper topspin you need to keep the ball high above the net and hit the ball below to brush up. The swing starts with the racket head below the ball. The topspin will keep the ball within the court as it will bounce down. Hitting to the corners is always safer as it gives you more court space.

Hitting aggressive strokes all the time is also a reflection of your inner feelings that are embedded in your subconscious. Perhaps there is a bit of anxiety about making an error or losing a point within you. You can get over it with deep breathing and believing that being aggressive is not a bad thing, you just need to give the feeling a controlled direction. Introspect. Playing slow does not constitute weakness. Playing a bit slower with consistency makes more sense in the long run. Playing a drop shot is also a way to win a point. To do that you need to be fit enough to run up to the net in case of a return drop shot. That takes us to the next point of the stance. You need to be constantly shifting your weight between your feet, balancing your weight and being ready to move in any direction. There are foot shuffling exercises that you can do to get your reflexes going.

"Concerning my mental balance during the game, whenever I try to play cautious or for points, or slowly I never cross the net."

This is a classic error most recreational players make. They tend to start a game without practising adequately. Devote three days a week to practice the shots that you would like to execute in a game. Do not be afraid to move up to the net. Practice your volleys and overhead smashes to gain confidence. The chapter on Practise addresses this point.

"I like to play more but my home situation doesn't allow it. So I sometimes think my wife will call me back home while playing which is also distracting."

A heart to heart conversation using the right environment should solve the issue. Perhaps your wife does not want to call you. Perhaps it is good for her to be on her own for a bit. We are talking about a max of 3 hours here, not like golf where you are gone for a day! Can you imagine what you would have faced as a golfer? Trust me I have been married for 40 years and have played both golf and tennis!

"During my learning phase, due to my childhood cricket skills I used to hit a lot of new balls outside our apartment Without getting into frustration, my friend used to teach me how to play topspin and how to control the shots. I was slowly learning the game and controlling my hits. I struggled to unlearn badminton and learn tennis. Due to that, I played a lot of wrist shots in Tennis. My friend slowly corrected me to point those mistakes. Till that time, I was serving very slowly. Again he corrected me to serve fast just by tossing the ball right height and hitting it at the maximum height and how to control balance after doing the serve. Which I could able to pick quickly and able to server nice aces."

Techniques used in other sports are bound to affect your tennis. That's ok as long as you are aware of the errors. Correct strokes for tennis needs to get into your muscle memory, and it will happen as you are playing more tennis than any other game. Yes, the toss and the point of contact with the ball, does make a big difference to the quality of your service.

Step into the court confident, assertive, cool and determined to enjoy yourself. If you want to play like a champion, you have to feel like a champion. No one plays well feeling angry, doubtful or insecure. Drop the past and the future, live the present moment on the court.

What may run in your mind is "I know that to play well I need to feel confident, but I can only gain confidence if I play well. But if I am not confident how can I play well?" It is the old chicken or the egg story.

CONCLUSION

It has been a pleasure writing this book and I hope you have managed to put into practice the teachings gathered over many years.

I sincerely hope I have been able to address all the angst faced by my fellow tennis players and have managed to drive home the point that happiness is our birthright and no individual or their action can displace it. Our existence on this planet is a game, let us treat it and play it like one.

Have a good game mates!

EPILOGUE

Going forward into the future it would be great to see professionals of all sports becoming equally competent in both the mental and the skill aspects of the game, and be able to guide the development of both in their students. This will add dignity to the players, their coaches and the sport.

Many youngsters with good potential do not come from a strong economic background. We need to see more tennis courts with subsidized tennis balls and rackets for school children. I am sure our country can produce more tennis players, let us give them a platform and encourage them. Please feel free to write to me on bobseshadri@yahoo.co.uk

ACKNOWLEDGEMENT

I value all the inputs given by my mates and recreational tennis players interviewed for the book. I hope I have been able to address them all.

Thank you Amuda Khanna and Axxelus Mavens for helping me design the book cover.

ABOUT THE AUTHOR

Bob Seshadri

Bob started playing tennis when he was 8 years old. He went on to win the under 13 and 18 years categories in the State of West Bengal, India. Unfortunately he ended up with multiple fractures on his left leg that placed him out of competitive tennis. After a long hospitalization, Bob continued to work in India and several other countries, coaching tennis in his free time and retired in 2014. Bob is a Management Consultant, plays and teaches tennis.

BOOKS BY THIS AUTHOR

Selling by Persuasion (The Gentle Art of Persuasion)

Why read this book?

After reading the book, the reader will excel in their career, with the acquired communication skills, they will also do well in their social circles by tried and tested techniques.

Today's customer has a high exposure of information available from the internet, has less time and limited patience. By the time the customer reaches the showroom after multiple interactions on the net, all he or she needs is crisp and clear information.

In this book the Consultant's speaking and listening skills are honed to reflect empathy, compassion and transparency, to overcome the barriers of apprehension in the customer.

The contents include skill development in promoting two-way communications, a win-win negotiation style, learning to qualify by understanding the need, presenting the product or services, and handling objections with confidence and closing the deal.

Set in the scenario of an unforgiving competitive automotive retail market environment, the takeaways from this book include understanding open-ended and closed questions with careful usage of the words what, when, why, where and how.

This book will help the reader achieve that excellence and set them apart from the rest of the crowd.

Work Life Balance in 30 Days

Why should you read and use this book?

Most of us find the avalanche of Emails, To-Dos, and stuff that pours down
from all directions quite nerve-racking, and end up with a 10 to 12-hour
routine.
☐ We feel they are organized but are we?
☐ How many important things fall off the table?
☐ How many intentions could not be acted upon?
☐ How many days since they had a family outing.
☐ Today we have all the gadgets, but still can't seem to manage work

within the 8 hours of a significantly large time frame.

This book will not only help you advance in your career using the techniques
that are taught, you will suddenly find yourself meeting deadlines well in
advance, with more time in your hands to do some creative thinking, go to the
gym, play some games, and be home on time to look after your personal and
family needs. This book will teach you to be super productive, using tried and
tested methods, and also reach a work-life balance that will leave you fulfilled.

Personal Journal

This is a 12-week journal, with a target to reach your destination within 4 weeks. You can use this journal along with https://www.amazon.com/Bobs-Guide-Work-Life-Balance-ebook/dp/B08Y6ZNQ1W or you may use it independently. The first page states how to use this journal. This journal will help you make the best use of your time. Pick out things that you want to prioritize and write them down. The page for evening reflections will help you review the day. Unfinished jobs are to be transferred to the next page. A habit of scheduling and writing down will go a long way in achieving efficiency in your work-place or home. Make time for your commitments. Do spend time reading and introspecting on the quotes. The last chapter summarizes 'Work-Life Balance'.

Printed in Great Britain
by Amazon

28306249R00086